Great-Tasting
LOW-CARB
RECIPES

Publications International, Ltd.
Favorite Brand Name Recipes at www.fbnr.com

Front cover photography and photography on pages 8, 25, 26, 28, 30, 46, 56, 66, 86, 92, 105, 106, 108, 112 and 120 by Chris Cassidy Photography, Inc.

Photographer: Chris Cassidy
Studio Manager: Nancy Cassidy
Photographer's Assistant: Marlene Rounds
Food Stylists: Lezli Bitterman, Stephanie Samuels

Pictured on the front cover: Pecan Catfish with Cranberry Compote *(page 66)*.
Pictured on the back cover *(left to right):* Individual Spinach & Bacon Quiche *(page 8)* and Pork & Peppers Mexican-Style *(page 46)*.

ISBN: 1-4127-2051-6

Manufactured in China.

8 7 6 5 4 3 2 1

Nutritional Analysis: The nutritional information that appears with each recipe was submitted in part by the participating companies and associations. Every effort has been made to check the accuracy of these numbers. However, because numerous variables account for a wide range of values for certain foods, nutritive analyses in this book should be considered approximate.

Microwave Cooking: Microwave ovens vary in wattage. Use the cooking times as guidelines and check for doneness before adding more time.

Preparation/Cooking Times: Preparation times are based on the approximate amount of time required to assemble the recipe before cooking, baking, chilling or serving. These times include preparation steps such as measuring, chopping and mixing. The fact that some preparations and cooking can be done simultaneously is taken into account. Preparation of optional ingredients and serving suggestions is not included.

Note: This book is for informational purposes and is not intended to provide medical advice. Neither Publications International, Ltd., nor the authors, editors or publisher take responsibility for any possible consequences from any treatment, procedure, exercise, dietary modification, action, or applications of medication or preparation by any person reading or following the information in this cookbook. The publication of this book does not constitute the practice of medicine, and this cookbook does not attempt to replace your physician or your pharmacist **Before undertaking any course of treatment, the authors, editors and publisher advise the reader to check with a physician or other health care provider.**

Contents

Start Out Strong

It's true—breakfast is the most important meal of the day, especially when you're dieting. Wake up to the luxurious low-carb flavor of an omelet or frittata, or for a change of pace, indulge in Deep South Ham and Redeye Gravy or Blueberry Cheesecake Muffins.

Deep South Ham and Redeye Gravy

1 tablespoon butter
1 ham steak (about 1⅓ pounds)
1 cup strong coffee
¾ teaspoon sugar
¼ teaspoon hot pepper sauce

1. Heat large skillet over medium-high heat until hot. Add butter; tilt skillet to coat bottom. Add ham steak; cook 3 minutes. Turn; cook 2 minutes longer or until lightly browned. Remove ham to serving platter; set aside and keep warm.

2. Add coffee, sugar and pepper sauce to same skillet. Bring to a boil over high heat; boil 2 to 3 minutes or until liquid is reduced to ¼ cup liquid, scraping up any brown bits. Serve gravy over ham.

Makes 4 servings

Serving Suggestion: Serve ham steak with sautéed greens and poached eggs.

Nutrients per Serving: Calories: 215, Total Fat: 9 g, Protein: 30 g, Carbohydrate: 1 g, Cholesterol: 76 mg, Sodium: 2 mg, Dietary Fiber: >1 g, Saturated Fat: 1g

A good breakfast will help keep you feeling satisfied. Meat, salads and even smoked fish are good low-carb choices in addition to eggs. If you're on the run with no time to cook, grab some cold cuts or a hard boiled egg so you won't be tempted later by high-carb breakfast sweets.

Individual Spinach & Bacon Quiches

3 strips bacon
½ small onion, diced
1 package (9 ounces) frozen chopped spinach, thawed, drained and squeezed dry
½ teaspoon pepper
⅛ teaspoon ground nutmeg
Pinch salt
1 container (15-ounces) whole milk ricotta cheese
2 cups (8 ounces) shredded mozzarella cheese
1 cup (4 ounces) grated Parmesan cheese
3 eggs, beaten slightly

1. Preheat oven to 350°F. Spray muffin pan with nonstick cooking spray.

2. Cook bacon in large skillet on medium-high heat until crisp. Drain, cool and crumble.

3. In same skillet cook and stir onion in remaining bacon fat 5 minutes or until tender. Add spinach, pepper, nutmeg and salt. Cook and stir over medium heat about 3 minutes or until liquid evaporates. Return bacon to skillet and remove from heat.

4. Combine ricotta, mozzarella and Parmesan cheese in large bowl; mix in eggs. Add cooled spinach mixture and combine well.

5. Divide mixture evenly to fill 10 muffin cups. Bake 40 minutes or until filling is set. Let stand 10 minutes. Run thin knife around edges to release. Serve hot or refrigerate and serve cold.

Makes 10 servings

Nutrients per Serving (1 quiche): Calories: 216, Total Fat: 15 g, Protein: 17 g, Carbohydrate: 4 g, Cholesterol: 105 mg, Sodium: 405 mg, Dietary Fiber: 1 g, Saturated Fat: 9g

Individual Spinach & Bacon Quiche

Feta Brunch Bake

1 medium red bell pepper
2 bags (10 ounces each) fresh spinach, washed and stemmed
6 eggs
6 ounces crumbled feta cheese
⅓ cup chopped onion
2 tablespoons chopped fresh parsley
¼ teaspoon dried dill weed
Dash black pepper

Preheat broiler. Place bell pepper on foil-lined broiler pan. Broil, 4 inches from heat, 15 to 20 minutes or until blackened on all sides, turning every 5 minutes with tongs. Place in paper bag; close bag and set aside to cool about 15 to 20 minutes. To peel pepper, cut around core, twist and remove. Cut in half and rub off skin; rinse under cold water. Cut into ½-inch pieces.

To blanch spinach, bring ½ cup water to a boil in Dutch oven. Add spinach; cover and cook 2 to 3 minutes until wilted. Drain and run cold water over colander to stop cooking. Drain; let stand until cool enough to handle. Squeeze spinach to remove excess water; finely chop.

Preheat oven to 400°F. Grease 1-quart baking dish. Beat eggs in large bowl with electric mixer at medium speed until foamy. Stir in bell pepper, spinach, cheese, onion, parsley, dill weed and black pepper. Pour egg mixture into prepared dish. Bake 20 minutes or until set. Let stand 5 minutes before serving. Garnish as desired.

Makes 4 servings

Nutrients per Serving: Calories: 266, Total Fat: 17 g, Protein: 20 g, Carbohydrate: 10 g, Cholesterol: 359 mg, Sodium: 684 mg, Dietary Fiber: 4 g, Saturated Fat: 9g

Feta Brunch Bake

Ham & Cheddar Frittata

        3 eggs
        3 egg whites
    ½ teaspoon salt
    ½ teaspoon freshly ground black pepper
  1½ cups (4 ounces) frozen broccoli florets, thawed
        6 ounces deli smoked ham, cut into ½-inch cubes (1¼ cups)
    ⅓ cup drained bottled roasted red bell peppers, cut into thin
        strips
    1 tablespoon butter
    ½ cup (2 ounces) shredded sharp Cheddar cheese

1. Preheat broiler.

2. Beat eggs, egg whites, salt and pepper in large bowl until blended. Stir in broccoli, ham and pepper strips.

3. Melt butter over medium heat in 10-inch ovenproof skillet with sloping side. Pour egg mixture into skillet; cover. Cook 5 to 6 minutes or until eggs are set around edge. (Center will be wet.)

4. Uncover; sprinkle cheese over frittata. Transfer skillet to broiler; broil, 5 inches from heat source, 2 minutes or until eggs are set in center and cheese is melted. Let stand 5 minutes; cut into wedges.

Makes 4 servings

Nutrients per Serving: Calories: 210, Total Fat: 13 g, Protein: 19 g, Carbohydrate: 5 g, Cholesterol: 201 mg, Sodium: 995 mg, Dietary Fiber: 1 g, Saturated Fat: 6g

Ham & Cheddar Frittata

Blueberry Cheesecake Muffins

8 ounces cream cheese, softened
1 cup plus 1 tablespoon sugar substitute for baking, divided
2 eggs
1 teaspoon grated lemon peel
1 teaspoon vanilla
¾ cup bran flakes cereal
½ cup all-purpose flour
½ cup soy flour
2 teaspoons baking powder
¼ teaspoon salt
¾ cup milk
3 tablespoons melted butter
4 tablespoons no-sugar-added blueberry fruit spread
½ teaspoon ground cinnamon

1. Preheat oven to 350°F. Spray 12 muffin cups with nonstick cooking spray.

2. Beat cream cheese in medium bowl at high speed of electric mixer until smooth. Beat in ¾ cup sugar substitute, 1 egg, lemon peel and vanilla.

3. Stir together cereal, flours, ¼ cup sugar substitute, baking powder and salt in medium bowl. In separate small bowl, whisk milk, butter and 1 egg until blended; pour over cereal mixture. Mix gently just until blended.

4. Spoon about 2 tablespoons batter into each muffin cup. Spread 1 teaspoon fruit spread over batter. Spread cream cheese mixture over fruit spread. Combine remaining 1 tablespoon sugar substitute and cinnamon; sprinkle mixture evenly over cream cheese mixture.

5. Bake 30 to 35 minutes or until toothpick inserted into centers comes out clean. Cool muffins 10 minutes in pan on wire rack. Remove muffins from pan and cool. Serve warm or at room temperature. Refrigerate leftover muffins.   *Makes 12 muffins*

Nutrients per Serving (1 muffin): Calories: 178, Total Fat: 11 g, Protein: 5 g, Carbohydrate: 14 g, Cholesterol: 66 mg, Sodium: 255 mg, Dietary Fiber: 1 g, Saturated Fat: 6g

Blueberry Cheesecake Muffins

Swiss Canadian Bacon & Eggs

8 eggs
¼ cup milk
½ teaspoon salt
¼ teaspoon black pepper
⅓ cup finely chopped green onions, divided
**   Nonstick cooking spray**
4 slices Canadian bacon, cut in half
1 cup (4 ounces) shredded Swiss cheese

1. Preheat broiler.

2. Whisk together eggs, milk, salt and pepper in medium bowl until well blended. Reserve 2 tablespoons onions. Stir in remaining onions.

3. Spray 12-inch ovenproof skillet with cooking spray; heat over medium-low heat until hot. Add egg mixture. Cover and cook 14 minutes or until almost set.

4. Arrange bacon in pinwheel on top of egg mixture. Sprinkle with cheese; broil 2 minutes or until cheese is bubbly. Top with reserved 2 tablespoons onions. Cut into 4 wedges. Serve immediately.

Makes 4 servings

Nutrients per Serving: Calories: 309, Total Fat: 20 g, Protein: 27 g, Carbohydrate: 4 g, Cholesterol: 466 mg, Sodium: 898 mg, Dietary Fiber: <1 g, Saturated Fat: 9g

Swiss Canadian Bacon & Eggs

Greek Isles Omelet

Nonstick cooking spray
¼ cup chopped onion
¼ cup canned artichoke hearts, rinsed and drained
¼ cup washed and torn spinach leaves
¼ cup chopped plum tomato
2 tablespoons sliced pitted ripe olives, rinsed and drained
1 cup cholesterol-free egg substitute
Dash black pepper

1. Spray small nonstick skillet with cooking spray; heat over medium heat until hot. Cook and stir onion 2 minutes or until crisp-tender.

2. Add artichoke hearts. Cook and stir until heated through. Add spinach, tomato and olives; toss briefly. Remove from heat. Transfer vegetables to small bowl. Wipe out skillet and spray with cooking spray.

3. Combine egg substitute and pepper in medium bowl. Heat skillet over medium heat until hot. Pour egg mixture into skillet. Cook over medium heat 5 to 7 minutes; as eggs begin to set, gently lift edge of omelet with spatula and tilt skillet so uncooked portion flows underneath.

4. When egg mixture is set, spoon vegetable mixture over half of omelet. Loosen omelet with spatula and fold in half. Slide omelet onto serving plate. *Makes 2 servings*

Nutrients per Serving: Calories: 111, Total Fat: 3 g, Protein: 13 g, Carbohydrate: 7 g, Cholesterol: 0 mg, Sodium: 538 mg, Dietary Fiber: 1 g, Saturated Fat: <1g

Greek Isles Omelet

Apple & Brie Omelet

2 large Golden Delicious apples
2 tablespoons butter or margarine, divided
½ teaspoon ground nutmeg
4 ounces Brie cheese
8 large eggs
2 green onions, thinly sliced

1. Place large serving platter in oven and preheat to 200°F. Peel, core and slice apples; place in microwavable container. Top with 1 tablespoon butter and nutmeg. Cover and microwave at HIGH (100% power) 3 minutes. Set aside. While apples cook, trim rind from cheese; thinly slice cheese.

2. Melt 1½ teaspoons butter in medium nonstick skillet over medium heat; rotate skillet to coat bottom. Place eggs in medium bowl and whisk until blended. Pour half of eggs into skillet. Let cook, without stirring, 1 to 2 minutes, or until set on bottom. With rubber spatula, lift side of omelet and slightly tilt pan to allow uncooked portion of egg to flow underneath. Cover pan and cook 2 to 3 minutes, until eggs are set but still moist on top. Remove platter from oven and slide omelet into center. Spread apples evenly over entire omelet, reserving a few slices for garnish, if desired. Evenly space cheese slices over apples. Sprinkle with onion, reserving some for garnish. Return platter to oven.

3. Cook remaining beaten eggs in remaining 1½ teaspoons butter as directed above. When cooked, slide spatula around edge to be certain omelet is loose. Carefully place second omelet over cheese, apple and onion mixture. Top with reserved apple and onion slices. Cut into wedges to serve. *Makes 4 servings*

Nutrients per Serving: Calories: 334, Total Fat: 24 g, Protein: 19 g, Carbohydrate: 11 g, Cholesterol: 469 mg, Sodium: 362 mg, Dietary Fiber: 1 g, Saturated Fat: 11g

Apple & Brie Omelet

Cheddary Sausage Frittata

4 eggs
¼ cup milk
1 package (12 ounces) bulk breakfast pork sausage
1 poblano pepper,* seeded and chopped
1 cup (4 ounces) shredded Cheddar cheese

1. Preheat broiler.

2. Combine eggs and milk in medium bowl; whisk until well blended. Set aside.

3. Heat 12-inch ovenproof nonstick skillet over medium-high heat until hot. Add sausage; cook and stir 4 minutes or until no longer pink, breaking up sausage with spoon. Drain sausage on paper towels; set aside.

4. Add pepper to same skillet; cook and stir 2 minutes or until crisp-tender. Return sausage to skillet. Add egg mixture and stir until blended. Cover and cook 10 minutes on medium-low or until eggs are almost set.

5. Sprinkle cheese over egg mixture; broil 2 minutes or until cheese is melted. Cut into 4 wedges. Serve immediately.   *Makes 4 servings*

Smart Tip: If skillet is not ovenproof, wrap handle in heavy-duty aluminum foil.

Nutrients per Serving: Calories: 498, Total Fat: 39 g, Protein: 24 g, Carbohydrate: 5 g, Cholesterol: 292 mg, Sodium: 673 mg, Dietary Fiber: <1g , Saturated Fat: 14 g

Cheddary Sausage Frittata

Savor Sensible Snacks

From Great Zukes Pizza Bites to elegant Smoked Salmon Roses, these recipes take snacking to a delicious new level. You'll find appetizer ideas as well as satisfying between-meal munchies. Low-carb has never been more full of flavor.

Parmesan-Pepper Crisps

2 cups (4 ounces) loosely packed coarsely-grated Parmesan cheese
2 teaspoons freshly grated black pepper

1. Preheat oven to 400°F.

2. Place heaping teaspoonfuls of cheese 2 inches apart on nonstick baking sheet. Spread the mounds of cheese with back of spoon to flatten. Sprinkle each mound with a pinch of pepper.

3. Bake 15 to 20 minutes until crisps are lightly colored. Watch closely as they burn easily. Let cool on baking pan 2 minutes; carefully remove with spatula to paper-towel lined rack. Store, refrigerated, up to 3 days in airtight container.

Makes about 26 crisps

Nutrients per Serving (1 crisp): Calories: 28, Total Fat: 2 g, Protein: 3 g, Carbohydrate: <1 g, Cholesterol: 5 mg, Sodium: 115 mg, Dietary Fiber: <1 g, Saturated Fat: 1 g

Smoked Salmon Roses

1 package (8 ounces) cream cheese, softened
1 tablespoon prepared horseradish
1 tablespoon minced fresh dill plus whole sprigs for garnish
1 tablespoon half-and-half
16 slices (12 to 16 ounces) smoked salmon
1 red bell pepper, cut into thin strips

1. Combine cream cheese, horseradish, minced dill and half-and-half in a bowl. Beat until light.

2. Spread 1 tablespoon cream cheese mixture over each salmon slice. Roll up jelly-roll fashion from the long end. Slice each roll in half widthwise. Stand salmon rolls, cut side up, on a serving dish to resemble roses. Garnish each "rose" by tucking 1 pepper strip and 1 dill sprig in center.   *Makes 32 servings*

Nutrients per Serving (1 "rose"): Calories: 40, Total Fat: 3 g, Protein: 3 g, Carbohydrate: 1 g, Cholesterol: 10 mg, Sodium: 106 mg, Dietary Fiber: <1 g, Saturated Fat: 2 g

When purchasing smoked salmon look for fish that looks fresh and isn't dried out around the edges. Sliced smoked salmon is available pre-packaged or from some delis. It is cold smoked. Nova is a shortened name for Nova Scotia salmon and generally refers to any cold-smoked salmon. Lox is brine-cured as well as smoked and is slightly saltier.

Smoked Salmon Roses

Great Zukes Pizza Bites

1 zucchini
3 tablespoons pizza sauce
2 tablespoons tomato paste
¼ teaspoon crushed dried oregano
¾ cup shredded reduced-fat mozzarella cheese
¼ cup shredded Parmesan cheese
8 pitted ripe olives
8 slices pepperoni

1. Preheat broiler and set rack 4 inches from heat.

2. Wash zucchini and trim off ends. Slice ¼-inch thick on diagonal to make 16 slices. Place zucchini over nonstick cookie sheet.

3. Stir pizza sauce, tomato paste and oregano together in cup. Spread scant teaspoon of sauce over each zucchini slice. Toss together mozzarella and Parmesan cheeses in small bowl. Top each zucchini slice with 1 tablespoon cheese mixture, pressing down into sauce. Arrange 1 olive on top of 8 pizza bites. Fold each pepperoni slice and place one on each remaining pizza bite.

4. Place cookie sheet under broiler and broil 3 minutes or until cheese melts and zucchini is tender. Remove from broiler and serve immediately.   *Makes 8 servings*

Nutrients per Serving (2 Pizza Bites): Calories: 75, Total Fat: 5 g, Protein: 5 g, Carbohydrate: 3 g, Cholesterol: 10 mg, Sodium: 288 mg, Dietary Fiber: 1 g, Saturated Fat: 2g

Great Zukes Pizza Bites

Rosemary-Scented Nut Mix

2 tablespoons unsalted butter
1 cup unsalted macadamia nuts
1 cup raw walnuts
2 cups raw pecan halves
½ teaspoon salt
1 teaspoon dried, crushed rosemary
¼ teaspoon crushed red pepper flakes

1. Preheat oven to 300°F. Melt butter in large pot. Add macadamia nuts, walnuts and pecans; stir well. Add salt, rosemary and red pepper flakes; stir over low heat 1 minute.

2. Pour nut mixture onto nonstick jelly-roll pan. Bake 15 minutes, shaking pan occasionally. Remove from oven and serve warm or at room temperature.   *Makes 32 servings*

Nutrients per Serving (2 tablespoons): Calories: 108, Total Fat: 11 g, Protein: 2 g, Carbohydrate: 2 g, Cholesterol: 2 mg, Sodium: 37 mg, Dietary Fiber: 1 g, Saturated Fat: 2g

Nuts are the perfect low-carb snack as long as you don't overdo. They're filling and contain healthy fats. You can adjust this recipe for Rosemary-Scented Nut Mix to your taste. Change the kinds of nuts or even the seasoning. Curry powder and chili powder are also excellent choices.

Rosemary-Scented Nut Mix

Jalapeño Wild Rice Cakes

⅓ cup wild rice
¾ cup water
½ teaspoon salt, divided
1 tablespoon all-purpose flour
½ teaspoon baking powder
1 egg
1 jalapeño pepper,* finely chopped
2 tablespoons minced onion
1 tablespoon freshly grated ginger *or* 2 teaspoons ground ginger
2 tablespoons vegetable or olive oil

*Jalapeño peppers can sting and irritate the skin; wear rubber gloves when handling peppers and do not touch eyes. Wash hands after handling.

1. Combine rice, water and ¼ teaspoon salt in medium saucepan. Bring to a boil. Reduce heat; cover and simmer 40 to 45 minutes or until rice is tender. Drain rice, if necessary; place in medium bowl. Add flour, baking powder and remaining ¼ teaspoon salt; mix until blended.

2. Whisk egg, jalapeño pepper, onion and ginger together in small bowl. Pour egg mixture over rice; mix until well blended.

3. Heat oil in large nonstick skillet over medium heat. Spoon 2 tablespoons rice mixture into pan and shape into cake. Cook, 4 cakes at a time, 3 minutes on each side or until golden brown. Transfer to paper towels. Serve immediately or refrigerate rice cakes for up to 24 hours.   *Makes 8 rice cakes*

Tip: To reheat cold rice cakes, preheat oven to 400°F. Place rice cakes in single layer on baking sheet; heat 5 minutes.

Nutrients per Serving (1 rice cake): Calories: 63, Total Fat: 4 g, Protein: 2 g, Carbohydrate: 5 g, Cholesterol: 27 mg, Sodium: 330 mg, Dietary Fiber: <1 g, Saturated Fat: 1g

Jalapeño Wild Rice Cakes

Cucumber Tomato Salad

½ cup rice vinegar*
3 tablespoons EQUAL® SPOONFUL**
3 cups unpeeled ¼-inch-thick sliced cucumbers, quartered
   (about 2 medium)
2 cups chopped tomato (about 1 large)
½ cup chopped red onion
   Salt and pepper to taste

*Distilled white vinegar can be substituted for rice vinegar.

**Can substitute 4½ packets Equal® sweetener.

• Combine vinegar and Equal®. Add cucumbers, tomato and onion. Season to taste with salt and pepper; mix well. Refrigerate, covered, at least 30 minutes before serving.   *Makes 6 servings*

Nutrients per Serving: Calories: 26, Total Fat: 0 g, Protein: 1 g, Carbohydrate: 6 g, Cholesterol: 0 mg, Sodium: 7 mg, Dietary Fiber: 1 g, Saturated Fat: 0g

Cucumbers provide crunch and that's something many low-carb snacks seem to lack. At only about 1 net carb gram per 1/2 cup of slices, there's no reason to limit them to salads. Try using cucumber slices as dippers, as a base for cream cheese and smoked salmon or just about anywhere you would use a cracker.

Cucumber Tomato Salad

Sesame Chicken Salad Wonton Cups

Nonstick cooking spray
20 (3-inch) wonton wrappers
1 tablespoon sesame seeds
2 cups water
2 small boneless skinless chicken breasts (about 8 ounces)
1 cup fresh green beans, cut diagonally into ½-inch pieces
¼ cup reduced-fat mayonnaise
1 tablespoon chopped fresh cilantro (optional)
2 teaspoons honey
1 teaspoon reduced-sodium soy sauce
⅛ teaspoon ground red pepper

1. Preheat oven to 350°F. Spray miniature muffin pan with cooking spray. Press 1 wonton wrapper into each muffin cup; spray with cooking spray. Bake 8 to 10 minutes or until golden brown. Cool in pan on wire rack before filling.

2. Place sesame seeds in shallow baking pan. Bake 5 minutes or until lightly toasted, stirring occasionally. Set aside to cool.

3. Meanwhile, bring water to a boil in medium saucepan. Add chicken. Reduce heat to low; cover. Simmer 10 minutes or until chicken is no longer pink in center, adding green beans after 7 minutes. Drain.

4. Finely chop chicken. Place in medium bowl. Add green beans and remaining ingredients; mix lightly. Spoon lightly rounded tablespoonful chicken mixture into each wonton cup. Garnish, if desired. *Makes 10 servings*

Nutrients per Serving (2 Wonton Cups): Calories: 103, Total Fat: 3 g, Protein: 7 g, Carbohydrate: 12 g, Cholesterol: 18 mg, Sodium: 128 mg, Dietary Fiber: <1 g, Saturated Fat: 1g

Sesame Chicken Salad Wonton Cups

Tortellini Kabobs with Pesto Ranch Dip

1 (16 ounce bag) frozen tortellini
1¼ cups ranch salad dressing
½ cup grated Parmesan cheese
3 cloves garlic, minced
2 teaspoons dried basil leaves

1. Cook tortellini according to package directions. Rinse and drain under cold water. Thread tortellini onto bamboo skewers, 2 tortellini per skewer.

2. Combine salad dressing, cheese, garlic and basil in small bowl. Serve tortellini kabobs with dip.   *Makes 6 to 8 servings*

Serving suggestion: For an even quicker dip, combine purchased spaghetti sauce or salsa with some finely chopped black olives.

Prep and Cook Time: 30 minutes

Nutrients per Serving: Calories: 288, Total Fat: 23 g, Protein: 8 g, Carbohydrate: 14 g, Cholesterol: 33 mg, Sodium: 585 mg, Dietary Fiber: >1, Saturated Fat: 6g

Tortellini Kabobs with Pesto Ranch Dip

Swimming Tuna Dip

1 cup low-fat (1%) cottage cheese
1 tablespoon reduced-fat mayonnaise
1 tablespoon lemon juice
2 teaspoons dry ranch-style salad dressing mix
1 can (3 ounces) chunk white tuna packed in water, drained
    and flaked
2 tablespoons sliced green onion or chopped celery
1 teaspoon dried parsley flakes
1 package (12 ounces) peeled baby carrots

Combine cottage cheese, mayonnaise, lemon juice and salad dressing mix in food processor or blender. Cover and blend until smooth. Combine tuna, green onion and parsley in small bowl. Stir in cottage cheese mixture. Serve with carrots.   *Makes 4 servings*

Nutrients per Serving: Calories: 116, Total Fat: 3 g, Protein: 13 g, Carbohydrate: 10 g, Cholesterol: 12 mg, Sodium: 449 mg, Dietary Fiber: 2 g, Saturated Fat: 1g

Swimming Tuna Dip

Peppered Shrimp Skewers

16 (12-inch) wooden skewers
⅓ cup teriyaki sauce
⅓ cup ketchup
2 tablespoons dry sherry or water
2 tablespoons reduced-fat peanut butter
1 teaspoon hot pepper sauce
¼ teaspoon ground ginger
32 fresh large shrimp (about 1½ pounds)
2 large yellow bell peppers
32 fresh sugar snap peas, trimmed

1. To prevent burning, soak skewers in water at least 20 minutes before assembling kabobs.

2. Coat rack of broiler pan with nonstick cooking spray; set aside.

3. Combine teriyaki sauce, ketchup, sherry, peanut butter, pepper sauce and ginger in small saucepan. Bring to a boil, stirring constantly. Reduce heat to low; simmer, uncovered, 1 minute. Remove from heat; set aside.

4. Peel and devein shrimp, leaving tails intact.

5. Cut each bell pepper lengthwise into 4 quarters; remove stems and seeds. Cut each quarter crosswise into 4 equal pieces. Thread 2 shrimp, bell pepper pieces and sugar snap peas onto each skewer; place on prepared broiler pan. Brush with teriyaki sauce mixture.

6. Broil 4 inches from heat 3 minutes; turn over. Brush with teriyaki sauce mixture; broil 2 minutes longer or until shrimp turn pink. Discard any remaining teriyaki sauce mixture. Transfer skewers to serving plates. *Makes 16 servings*

Nutrients per Serving (1 Skewer): Calories: 69, Total Fat: 1 g, Protein: 8 g, Carbohydrate: 6 g, Cholesterol: 66 mg, Sodium: 258 mg, Dietary Fiber: 1 g, Saturated Fat: <1g

Peppered Shrimp Skewer

Eating Right Entrées

It's hard to believe these luscious main courses, including Jalapeño-Lime Chicken and Two Cheese Sausage Pizza, are all under 15 grams of carbs per serving, but they are. With recipes that are this satisfying you never have to feel deprived.

Parmesan Turkey Breast

½ **teaspoon salt**
¼ **teaspoon freshly ground black pepper**
1 **pound turkey breast, chicken breast or veal cutlets, cut**
    ⅛- **to** ¼-**inch thick**
2 **tablespoons butter, melted**
2 **cloves garlic, minced**
½ **cup grated Parmesan cheese**
1 **cup spicy marinara sauce or mushroom or olive pasta**
    sauce, warmed
2 **tablespoons chopped fresh basil or Italian parsley**

Preheat broiler. Sprinkle salt and pepper over turkey. Place turkey in 1 layer in a 15×10-inch jelly-roll pan. Combine butter and garlic; brush over turkey. Broil 4 to 5 inches from heat source for 2 minutes; turn. Top with cheese. Continue to broil 2 to 3 minutes or until turkey is no longer pink in center. Transfer to serving plates; spoon sauce over turkey and top with basil.   *Makes 4 servings*

Variation: Alternatively, preheat oven to 350°F. Sprinkle salt and pepper over turkey. Brown turkey on both sides in 1 to 2 tablespoons hot oil in a medium skillet. Place browned turkey in a small casserole or 9×9-inch baking dish. Top with pasta sauce, cover pan with foil, and bake until no longer pink in center, about 30 minutes. Remove from oven and remove foil; sprinkle with Parmesan cheese and basil.

Nutrients per Serving: Calories: 251, Total Fat: 10 g, Protein: 33 g, Carbohydrate: 5 g, Cholesterol: 95 mg, Sodium: 832 mg, Dietary Fiber: 2 g, Saturated Fat: 6 g

Pork & Peppers Mexican-Style

2 tablespoons olive oil
½ cup chopped green onions
¾ pound lean pork, cut into ¼-inch pieces
3 bell peppers, preferably red, green and yellow, diced
   (about 2 cups)
1 teaspoon chopped garlic
   Salt and pepper
1 cup sliced fresh mushrooms
1 teaspoon cumin
1 teaspoon chili powder
½ teaspoon ground dried chipotle pepper (optional)
¼ cup shredded Cheddar cheese
¼ cup sour cream

1. Heat oil in large skillet over medium high heat. Add green onions; cook and stir 2 minutes. Add pork; cook and stir 5 minutes or until browned. Add peppers and garlic. Cook and stir 5 minutes or until peppers begin to soften.

2. Season with salt and pepper. Add mushrooms, cumin, chili powder and chipotle pepper, if desired. Cook and stir 10 to 15 minutes until pork is cooked through and vegetables have softened.

3. Serve topped with shredded cheese and sour cream.

Makes 4 servings

Tip: Those not restricting carbohydrates can enjoy this dish rolled-up in tortillas, burrito-style.

Nutrients per Serving: Calories: 271, Total Fat: 17 g, Protein: 22 g, Carbohydrate: 9 g, Cholesterol: 63 mg, Sodium: 98 mg, Dietary Fiber: 3 g, Saturated Fat: 6 g

Pork & Peppers Mexican-Style

Blue Cheese-Stuffed Sirloin Patties

1½ pounds ground beef sirloin
½ cup (2 ounces) shredded sharp Cheddar cheese
¼ cup crumbled blue cheese
¼ cup finely chopped parsley
2 teaspoons Dijon mustard
1 teaspoon Worcestershire sauce
1 clove garlic, minced
¼ teaspoon salt
2 teaspoons olive oil
1 medium red bell pepper, cut into thin strips

1. Shape beef into 8 patties, about 4 inches in diameter and ¼ inch thick.

2. Combine cheeses, parsley, mustard, Worcestershire sauce, garlic and salt in small bowl; toss gently to blend.

3. Mound ¼ cheese mixture on 4 patties (about 3 tablespoons per patty). Top with remaining 4 patties; pinch edges of patties to seal completely. Set aside.

4. Heat oil in 12-inch nonstick skillet over medium-high heat until hot. Add pepper strips; cook and stir until edges of peppers begin to brown. Sprinkle with salt. Remove from skillet and keep warm.

5. Add beef patties to same skillet; cook on medium-high 5 minutes. Turn patties; top with peppers. Cook 4 minutes or until patties are no longer pink in centers (160°F).   *Makes 4 servings*

Nutrients per Serving: Calories: 463, Total Fat: 32 g, Protein: 38 g, Carbohydrate: 3 g, Cholesterol: 131 mg, Sodium: 548 mg, Dietary Fiber: 1 g, Saturated Fat: 16g

Blue Cheese-Stuffed Sirloin Patty

Lemon-Capered Pork Tenderloin

1 to 2 boneless pork tenderloins (about 1½ pounds)
1 tablespoon crushed capers
1 teaspoon dried rosemary leaves, crushed
⅛ teaspoon black pepper
1 cup water
¼ cup lemon juice

1. Preheat oven to 350°F. Trim fat from tenderloin; discard. Set tenderloin aside.

2. Combine capers, rosemary and black pepper in small bowl. Rub mixture over tenderloin. Place tenderloin in shallow roasting pan. Pour water and lemon juice over tenderloin.

3. Bake, uncovered, about 20 minutes or until thermometer inserted into thickest part of tenderloin registers 160°F. Remove from oven; cover with foil. Allow to stand 10 minutes. Cut into slices before serving. Garnish as desired. *Makes 8 servings*

Nutrients per Serving: Calories: 114, Total Fat: 3 g, Protein: 19 g, Carbohydrate: <1 g, Cholesterol: 45 mg, Sodium: 59 mg, Dietary Fiber: <1 g, Saturated Fat: 1 g

Capers are the flower buds of a Mediterranean bush. They are usually sold in jars pickled in brine. Try adding capers to low-carb egg and meat dishes and sauces for a unique, piquant flavor boost. Capers should be rinsed in a colander before using to make them less salty.

Lemon-Capered Pork Tenderloin

Broccoli-Filled Chicken Roulade

2 cups broccoli florets
1 tablespoon water
¼ cup fresh parsley
1 cup diced red bell pepper
4 ounces fat-free cream cheese, softened
2 tablespoons grated Parmesan cheese
2 tablespoons lemon juice
2 tablespoons olive oil
1 teaspoon paprika
¼ teaspoon salt
1 egg
½ cup fat-free (skim) milk
4 cups cornflakes, crushed
1 tablespoon dried basil leaves
8 boneless skinless chicken breast halves

1. Place broccoli and water in microwavable dish; cover. Microwave at HIGH 2 minutes. Let stand, covered, 2 minutes. Drain water from broccoli. Place broccoli in food processor or blender. Add parsley; process 10 seconds, scraping side of bowl if necessary. Add bell pepper, cream cheese, Parmesan cheese, lemon juice, oil, paprika and salt. Pulse 2 to 3 times or until bell pepper is minced.

2. Preheat oven to 375°F. Spray 11×7-inch baking pan with nonstick cooking spray. Lightly beat egg in small bowl. Add milk; blend well. Place cornflake crumbs in shallow bowl. Add basil; blend well.

3. Pound chicken breasts between two pieces of plastic wrap to ¼-inch thickness using flat side of meat mallet or rolling pin. Spread each chicken breast with ⅛ of broccoli mixture, spreading to within ½ inch of edges. Roll up chicken breast from short end, tucking in sides if possible; secure with toothpicks. Dip roulades in milk mixture; roll in cornflake crumb mixture. Place in prepared baking

pan. Bake 20 minutes or until chicken is no longer pink in center and juices run clear. Garnish, if desired. *Makes 8 servings*

Nutrients per Serving: Calories: 269, Total Fat: 8 g, Protein: 33 g, Carbohydrate: 15 g, Cholesterol: 103 mg, Sodium: 407 mg, Dietary Fiber: 2 g, Saturated Fat: 2 g

Broccoli-Filled Chicken Roulade

Bolognese-Style Pork Ragú over Spaghetti Squash

1½ pounds ground pork
1 cup finely chopped celery
½ cup chopped onion
1 teaspoon prepared crushed garlic *or* 2 cloves garlic, minced
2 tablespoons tomato paste
1 teaspoon Italian seasoning
1 can (14½ ounces) low-sodium chicken broth
½ cup half-and-half
1 spaghetti squash (3 to 4 pounds)
½ cup grated Parmesan (optional)

1. Brown pork in 3-quart saucepan over medium-high heat, stirring to break up meat. Add celery and onion; cook and stir 5 minutes over medium heat or until vegetables are tender. Add garlic, cook and stir 1 minute. Stir in tomato paste and Italian seasoning.

2. Stir in broth. Reduce heat. Simmer 10 to 15 minutes, stirring occasionally.

3. Add half-and-half; cook and stir until hot. Skim off excess fat.

4. Meanwhile, pierce spaghetti squash several times with knife. Microwave at HIGH (100%) 15 minutes until squash is tender (squash will yield when pressed with finger). Let cool 10 to 15 minutes. Cut in half, scoop out and discard seeds. Separate flesh into strands with fork; keep squash warm.

5. Serve ½ cup meat sauce over 1 cup spaghetti squash. Sprinkle with 1 tablespoon grated Parmesan, if desired.   *Makes 8 servings*

Tip: Sauce can be cooked the day before and refrigerated so that chilled fat can be easily removed and discarded before reheating.

Nutrients per Serving: Calories: 333, Total Fat: 22 g, Protein: 20 g, Carbohydrate: 15 g, Cholesterol: 75 mg, Sodium: 275 mg, Dietary Fiber: 2 g, Saturated Fat: 20 g

Bolognese-Style Pork Ragú over Spaghetti Squash

Two-Cheese Sausage Pizza

1 pound sweet Italian turkey sausage
1 tablespoon olive oil
1 small red onion, thinly sliced
2 cups sliced mushrooms
1 small green bell pepper, cut into thin strips
¼ teaspoon dried oregano leaves
¼ teaspoon salt
¼ teaspoon pepper
½ cup pizza sauce
2 tablespoons tomato paste
½ cup shredded Parmesan cheese
1 cup shredded reduced-fat mozzarella cheese
8 pitted ripe olives

1. Preheat oven to 400 F°. Remove turkey from casings. Pat into greased 9-inch glass pie plate. Bake for 10 minutes or until sausage is firm. Remove from oven and carefully pour off fat. Set aside.

2. Heat oil in large skillet. Add onion, mushrooms, bell pepper, oregano, salt and pepper. Cook and stir over medium-high heat 10 minutes or until vegetables are very tender and no longer give off any liquid.

3. Stir pizza sauce and tomato paste together in small bowl. Spread over turkey crust. Spoon half of vegetables over tomato sauce. Sprinkle on Parmesan and mozzarella cheeses. Top with remaining vegetables. Garnish with olives. Bake for 8 to 10 minutes or until cheese melts.   *Makes 4 servings*

Nutrients per Serving: Calories: 507, Total Fat: 43 g, Protein: 27 g, Carbohydrate: 11 g, Cholesterol: 78 mg, Sodium: 1249 mg, Dietary Fiber: 3 g, Saturated Fat: 15 g

Two-Cheese Sausage Pizza

Pork Chops Paprikash

2 teaspoons butter
1 medium onion, very thinly sliced
1¼ teaspoons paprika, divided
1 teaspoon garlic salt
½ teaspoon black pepper
4 (5- to 6-ounce) bone-in center-cut pork chops (about
     ½ inch thick)
⅓ cup well-drained sauerkraut
⅓ cup light or regular sour cream

1. Preheat broiler.

2. Melt butter in large skillet over medium-high heat. Separate onion slices into rings; add to skillet. Cook, stirring occasionally, until golden brown and tender, about 10 minutes.

3. Meanwhile, sprinkle 1 teaspoon paprika, garlic salt and pepper over both sides of pork chops. Place chops on rack of broiler pan.

4. Broil, 4 to 5 inches from heat source, 5 minutes. Turn; broil 4 to 5 minutes or until chops are barely pink in center.

5. Combine cooked onion with sauerkraut, sour cream and remaining ¼ teaspoon paprika; mix well. Garnish chops with onion mixture, or spread onion mixture over chops and return to broiler. Broil just until hot, about 1 minute.   *Makes 4 servings*

Nutrients per Serving: Calories: 216, Total Fat: 9 g, Protein: 27 g, Carbohydrate: 5 g, Cholesterol: 83 mg, Sodium: 420 mg, Dietary Fiber: 1 g, Saturated Fat: 4 g

Pork Chop Paprikash

Jalapeño-Lime Chicken

8 chicken thighs
3 tablespoons jalapeño jelly
1 tablespoon olive oil
1 tablespoon lime juice
1 clove garlic, minced
1 teaspoon chili powder
½ teaspoon black pepper
⅛ teaspoon salt

1. Preheat oven to 400°F. Line 15×10-inch jell-roll pan with foil; spray with nonstick cooking spray.

2. Arrange chicken in single layer in prepared pan. Bake 15 minutes; drain off juices. Combine jelly, oil, lime juice, garlic, chili powder, pepper and salt in small bowl. Turn chicken; brush with half of jelly mixture. Bake 20 minutes. Turn chicken; brush with remaining jelly mixture. Bake chicken 10 to 15 minutes or until juices run clear (180°F).   *Makes 8 servings*

Prep Time: 10 minutes
Cook Time: 55 minutes

Nutrients per Serving: Calories: 467, Total Fat: 32 g, Protein: 33 g, Carbohydrate: 11 g, Cholesterol: 158 mg, Sodium: 221 mg, Dietary Fiber: <1 g, Saturated Fat: 9 g

Jalapeño-Lime Chicken

One Pan Pork Fu Yung

1 cup fat-free reduced-sodium chicken broth
½ teaspoon sesame oil, divided
1 tablespoon cornstarch
2 teaspoons canola oil
½ pound boneless pork tenderloin, minced
5 green onions, thinly sliced, divided
1 cup sliced mushrooms
¼ teaspoon salt (optional)
¼ teaspoon white pepper
1 cup bean sprouts
2 eggs
2 egg whites

1. Combine broth, ¼ teaspoon sesame oil and cornstarch in small pan. Cook over medium heat, stirring, until sauce thickens, about 5 to 6 minutes. Set aside.

2. Heat canola oil in 12-inch nonstick skillet over high heat. Add pork; stir-fry about 4 minutes or until no longer pink.

3. Reserve 2 tablespoons green onions. Add remaining green onions, remaining ¼ teaspoon sesame oil, mushrooms, salt, if desired, and pepper to skillet. Cook and stir about 4 to 5 minutes or until lightly browned. Add sprouts to skillet; stir-fry about 1 minute. With spatula, flatten mixture in skillet.

4. Combine eggs and egg whites in medium bowl; pour over pork mixture in skillet. Reduce heat to low. Cover; cook about 3 minutes or until eggs are set.

5. Cut into 4 wedges before serving. Top each wedge with ¼ cup sauce and some of reserved 2 tablespoons green onions.

Makes 4 servings

To round it out: Serve with Lettuce Wrap Salad. Separate Boston lettuce leaves and arrange on a platter with grated carrot, radish sticks, seedless cucumber rounds, red bell pepper strips and bean sprouts. Serve with a dipping sauce made by whisking together 1 cup fat-free reduced-sodium chicken broth, 1 tablespoon rice vinegar, ¼ teaspoon sesame oil, ¼ teaspoon minced ginger and ¼ teaspoon minced garlic. Serve dressing in small dishes for dipping.

Nutrients per Serving (1 wedge with ¼ cup sauce): Calories: 189, Total Fat: 9 g, Protein: 22 g, Carbohydrate: 6 g, Cholesterol: 149 mg, Sodium: 150 mg, Dietary Fiber: <1 g, Saturated Fat: 2 g

One Pan Pork Fu Yung

Get in the Swim

Seafood dishes add variety and good nutrition to low-carb eating. Dive into Pecan Catfish with Cranberry Compote or Caribbean Sea Bass with Mango Salsa. These easy recipes make it a cinch to lure the whole family to the table.

Grilled Salmon Fillets, Asparagus and Onions

½ teaspoon paprika
6 salmon fillets (6 to 8 ounces each)
⅓ cup bottled honey-Dijon marinade or barbecue sauce
1 bunch (about 1 pound) fresh asparagus spears, ends trimmed
1 large red or sweet onion, cut into ¼-inch slices
1 tablespoon olive oil
Salt and black pepper

1. Prepare grill for direct grilling. Sprinkle paprika over salmon fillets. Brush marinade over salmon; let stand at room temperature 15 minutes.

2. Brush asparagus and onion slices with olive oil; season to taste with salt and pepper.

3. Place salmon, skin side down, in center of grid over medium coals. Arrange asparagus spears and onion slices around salmon. Grill salmon and vegetables on covered grill 5 minutes. Turn salmon, asparagus and onion slices. Grill 5 to 6 minutes more or until salmon flakes easily when tested with a fork and vegetables are crisp-tender. Separate onion slices into rings; arrange over asparagus.

Makes 6 servings

Prep and Cook Time: 26 minutes

Nutrients per Serving: Calories: 255, Total Fat: 8 g, Protein: 35 g, Carbohydrate: 8 g, Cholesterol: 86 mg, Sodium: 483 mg, Dietary Fiber: 2 g, Saturated Fat: 1 g

Pecan Catfish with Cranberry Compote

Cranberry Compote (recipe follows)
1½ cups pecans
2 tablespoons flour
1 egg
2 tablespoons water
4 catfish fillets (about 1¼ pounds)
Salt and pepper
2 tablespoons butter, divided

1. Prepare Cranberry Compote and refrigerate at least 3 hours and up to several days in advance.

2. Preheat oven to 425°F. Place pecans and flour in bowl of food processor; pulse until finely chopped. *Do not overprocess or you may create nut butter.*

3. Place pecan mixture in shallow dish or plate; whisk egg and water in another shallow dish. Salt and pepper both sides of each fillet and dip first in egg mixture, then in pecans, pressing to make coating stick. Meanwhile, prepare baking pan. Place one tablespoon butter in 13×9-inch pan. Melt butter on stovetop or in oven and tilt to distribute evenly.

4. Place fillets in prepared pan. Top with pieces of remaining 1 tablespoon butter. Bake 15 to 20 minutes or until fish begins to flake when tested with fork. Serve with Cranberry Compote.

Makes 4 servings

Nutrients per Serving (1 fillet, plus ½ cup cranberry compote):
Calories: 305, Total Fat: 21 g, Protein: 16 g, Carbohydrate: 16 g, Cholesterol: 101 mg, Sodium: 97 mg, Dietary Fiber: 4 g, Saturated Fat: 4 g

Cranberry Compote

1 bag (12 ounces) cranberries
¾ cup water
½ cup sucralose-based sugar substitute
¼ cup orange juice
2 tablespoons dark brown sugar
2 teaspoons grated fresh ginger
¼ teaspoon five-spice powder
⅛ teaspoon salt
1 teaspoon butter

1. Wash and pick over cranberries, discarding any bad ones. Combine cranberries and all remaining ingredients except butter in large saucepan. Heat over medium high heat, stirring occasionally about 10 minutes or until berries begin to pop.

2. Cook and stir 5 minutes or until saucy consistency is reached. Remove from heat; stir in butter. Allow to cool; refrigerate until cold. Compote keeps up to 1 week under refrigeration.

Makes 8 servings

Pecan Catfish with Cranberry Compote

Trout Stuffed with Fresh Mint and Orange

2 pan-dressed* trout (1 to 1¼ pounds each)
½ teaspoon coarse salt, such as Kosher salt
1 orange, sliced
1 cup fresh mint leaves
1 sweet onion, sliced

*A pan-dressed trout has been gutted and scaled with head and tail removed.

1. Rinse trout under cold running water; pat dry with paper towels.

2. Sprinkle cavities of trout with salt; fill each with orange slices and mint. Cover each fish with onion slices.

3. Spray 2 large sheets of foil with nonstick cooking spray. Place 1 fish on each sheet and seal using drugstore wrap technique.**

4. Place foil packets, seam side down, directly on medium-hot coals; grill on covered grill 20 to 25 minutes or until trout flakes easily when tested with fork, turning once.

5. Carefully open foil packets, avoiding hot steam; remove and discard orange-mint stuffing. Serve immediately.

Makes 6 servings

**Place the food in the center of an oblong piece of heavy-duty foil, leaving at least a two-inch border around the food. Bring the two long sides together above the food; fold down in a series of locked folds, allowing for heat circulation and expansion. Fold the short ends up and over again. Press folds firmly to seal the foil packet.

Nutrients per Serving: Calories: 203, Total Fat: 5 g, Protein: 32 g, Carbohydrate: 5 g, Cholesterol: 87 mg, Sodium: 220 mg, Dietary Fiber: 1 g, Saturated Fat: 1 g

Trout Stuffed with Fresh Mint and Orange

Blackened Sea Bass

2 teaspoons paprika
1 teaspoon garlic salt
1 teaspoon dried thyme leaves, crushed
¼ teaspoon white pepper
¼ teaspoon ground red pepper
¼ teaspoon black pepper
3 tablespoons butter or margarine
4 skinless sea bass or catfish fillets (4 to 6 ounces each)
Lemon halves
Fresh dill sprigs for garnish

1. Prepare barbecue grill for direct cooking.

2. Meanwhile, combine paprika, garlic salt, thyme and white, red and black peppers in small bowl; mix well. Set aside. Melt butter in small saucepan over medium heat. Pour melted butter into pie plate or shallow bowl. Cool slightly.

3. Dip sea bass into melted butter, evenly coating both sides. Sprinkle both sides of sea bass evenly with paprika mixture.

4. Place sea bass on oiled grid. (Fire will flare up when sea bass is placed on grid, but will subside when grill is covered.) Grill sea bass, on covered grill, over hot coals 4 to 6 minutes or until sea bass is blackened and flakes easily when tested with fork, turning halfway through grilling time. Serve with lemon halves. Garnish, if desired.

Makes 4 serving

Nutrients per Serving: Calories: 195, Total Fat: 12 g, Protein: 21 g, Carbohydrate: 1 g, Cholesterol: 71 mg, Sodium: 411 mg, Dietary Fiber: >1 g, Saturated Fat: 6 g

Blackened Sea Bass

Poached Seafood Italiano

1 tablespoon olive or vegetable oil
1 large clove garlic, minced
¼ cup dry white wine or chicken broth
4 (6-ounce) salmon steaks or fillets
1 can (14.5 ounces) CONTADINA® Recipe Ready Diced
   Tomatoes with Italian Herbs, undrained
⅓ cup sliced olives (black, green or a combination)
2 tablespoons chopped fresh basil (optional)

1. Heat oil in large skillet. Add garlic; sauté 30 seconds. Add wine. Bring to boil.

2. Add salmon; cover. Reduce heat to medium; simmer 6 minutes.

3. Add undrained tomatoes and olives; simmer 2 minutes or until salmon flakes easily when tested with fork. Sprinkle with basil just before serving, if desired.   *Makes 4 servings*

Nutrients per Serving: Calories: 251, Total Fat: 9 g, Protein: 34 g, Carbohydrate: 5 g, Cholesterol: 86 mg, Sodium: 620 mg, Dietary Fiber: 1 g, Saturated Fat: 1 g

To poach is simply to cook gently in liquid. It's a quick and easy way to cook healthy, low-carb fish. Some of the flavor from the poaching liquid penetrates the fish and makes a delicious sauce. Be careful to lower the heat until the water is just quivering, but not boiling, or the fish could break apart.

Poached Seafood Italiano

Pineapple Salsa Topped Halibut

PINEAPPLE SALSA

- ¾ cup diced fresh pineapple *or* 1 can (8 ounces) unsweetened pineapple chunks, drained
- 2 tablespoons finely chopped red bell pepper
- 2 tablespoons chopped fresh cilantro
- 2 teaspoons vegetable oil
- 1 teaspoon minced ginger
- 1 teaspoon bottled minced jalapeño pepper or fresh jalapeño pepper*

HALIBUT

- 4 halibut or swordfish steaks (6 ounces each), cut about ¾-inch thick
- 1 tablespoon garlic-flavored olive oil**
- ¼ teaspoon salt

Jalapeño peppers can sting and irritate the skin; wear rubber gloves when handling peppers and do not touch eyes. Wash hands after handling.

**Or, add ¼ teaspoon bottled minced garlic to 1 tablespoon olive oil.*

1. For salsa, combine pineapple, bell pepper, cilantro, oil, ginger and jalapeño pepper in small bowl; mix well. Cover; refrigerate up to 2 days.

2. To complete recipe, prepare barbecue grill for direct cooking. Brush halibut with oil; sprinkle with salt.

3. Grill halibut, on uncovered grill, over medium-hot coals 8 minutes or until halibut flakes easily when tested with fork, turning once.

4. Top halibut with salsa; serve immediately.   *Makes 4 servings*

Nutrients per Serving: Calories: 253, Total Fat: 10 g, Protein: 36 g, Carbohydrate: 4 g, Cholesterol: 55 mg, Sodium: 237 mg, Dietary Fiber: <1 g, Saturated Fat: 1 g

Pineapple Salsa Topped Halibut

Red Snapper Vera Cruz

4 red snapper fillets (about 1 pound)
¼ cup fresh lime juice
1 tablespoon fresh lemon juice
1 teaspoon chili powder
4 green onions with 4 inches of tops, sliced in ½-inch lengths
1 tomato, coarsely chopped
½ cup chopped Anaheim or green bell pepper
½ cup chopped red bell pepper
Black pepper

Microwave Directions

1. Place red snapper in shallow 9- to 10-inch round microwavable baking dish. Combine lime juice, lemon juice and chili powder in small bowl. Pour over snapper. Marinate 10 minutes, turning once or twice.

2. Sprinkle green onions, tomato, Anaheim and bell pepper over snapper. Season with black pepper. Cover dish loosely with vented plastic wrap. Microwave at HIGH 5 to 6 minutes or just until snapper flakes in center, rotating dish every 2 minutes. Let stand, covered, 4 minutes. *Makes 4 servings*

Prep and Cook Time: 22 minutes

Nutrients per Serving (1 fillet with about ½ cup salsa): Calories: 144, Total Fat: 2 g, Protein: 24 g, Carbohydrate: 7 g, Cholesterol: 42 mg, Sodium: 61 mg, Dietary Fiber: 2 g, Saturated Fat: <1 g

Red Snapper Vera Cruz

Caribbean Sea Bass with Mango Salsa

4 skinless sea bass fillets (4 ounces each), about 1 inch thick
1 teaspoon Caribbean jerk seasoning
   Nonstick cooking spray
1 ripe mango, peeled, pitted and diced, *or* 1 cup diced
      drained bottled mango
2 tablespoons chopped fresh cilantro
2 teaspoons fresh lime juice
1 teaspoon minced jalapeño pepper*

*Jalapeño peppers can sting and irritate the skin; wear rubber gloves when handling peppers and do not touch eyes. Wash hands after handling.

1. Prepare grill or preheat broiler. Sprinkle fish with seasoning; coat lightly with cooking spray. Grill fish over medium coals or broil 5 inches from heat 4 to 5 minutes per side or until fish flakes easily when tested with fork.

2. Meanwhile, combine mango, cilantro, lime juice and jalapeño pepper in small bowl; mix well. Serve salsa over fish.

Makes 4 servings

Prep Time: 10 minutes
Cook Time: 8 minutes

Nutrients per Serving (1 fillet with about ¼ cup Mango Salsa):
Calories: 146, Total Fat: 3 g, Protein: 21 g, Carbohydrate: 9 g, Cholesterol: 47 mg, Sodium: 189 mg, Dietary Fiber: 1 g, Saturated Fat: 1 g

Caribbean Sea Bass with Mango Salsa

Mediterranean Mahimahi with Creamy Herb Sauce

Creamy Herb Sauce (recipe follows)
¼ cup lemon juice
2 tablespoons olive oil
1½ teaspoons grated lemon peel
½ teaspoon dried oregano leaves
¼ teaspoon salt
¼ teaspoon black pepper
1¼ pounds mahimahi, ½ to ¾ inch thick, cut into 4 or 5 pieces

Prepare Creamy Herb Sauce; cover and refrigerate.

Combine lemon juice, oil, lemon peel, oregano, salt and pepper in small bowl until blended. Place juice mixture and mahimahi in large resealable plastic food storage bag. Close bag securely, turning to coat. Marinate in refrigerator 30 minutes, turning after 15 minutes.

Prepare grill for direct cooking.

Drain mahimahi; reserve marinade. Place mahimahi on oiled grid. Grill, covered, over medium-high heat 4 to 5 minutes; turn and brush with reserved marinade. Grill 4 to 5 minutes or until mahimahi flakes easily when tested with fork. Serve with Creamy Herb Sauce.

Makes 4 to 5 servings

Nutrients per Serving: Calories: 208, Total Fat: 8 g, Protein: 28 g, Carbohydrate: 4 g, Cholesterol: 105 mg, Sodium: 278 mg, Dietary Fiber: <1 g, Saturated Fat: 1 g

Creamy Herb Sauce

½ **cup plain yogurt**
½ **cup chopped peeled cucumber**
1 **tablespoon chopped fresh basil**
1 **teaspoon dried oregano leaves**
½ **teaspoon dried mint leaves**
¼ **teaspoon minced garlic**
3 **dashes ground red pepper**

Combine all ingredients in small bowl until blended. Cover and refrigerate 1 hour before serving. *Makes about 1 cup*

Mediterranean Mahimahi with Creamy Herb Sauce

81

Today's Slim Tuna Stuffed Tomatoes

6 medium tomatoes
1 cup dry curd cottage cheese
½ cup plain low fat yogurt
1 can (6½ ounces) tuna, packed in water, drained and flaked
¼ cup chopped cucumber
¼ cup chopped green bell pepper
¼ cup thinly sliced radishes
¼ cup chopped green onions
½ teaspoon dried basil leaves
⅛ teaspoon garlic powder
  Lettuce leaves

Cut each tomato into 6 wedges, cutting to, but not through, base of each tomato. Refrigerate. In medium bowl, combine cottage cheese and yogurt; mix well. Stir in remaining ingredients except lettuce leaves. Place tomatoes on individual lettuce-lined plates; spread wedges apart. Spoon cottage cheese mixture into center of each tomato. *Makes 6 servings*

Favorite recipe from **Wisconsin Milk Marketing Board**

Nutrients per Serving (1 Stuffed Tomato): Calories: 98, Total Fat: 1 g, Protein: 14 g, Carbohydrate: 9 g, Cholesterol: 8 mg, Sodium: 48 mg, Dietary Fiber: 2 g, Saturated Fat: <1 g, Saturated Fat: <1 g

Today's Slim Tuna Stuffed Tomatoes

Shape Up Dinnertime

Enjoy low-carb versions of old favorites with recipes for Low-Carb Lasagna and Roast Turkey Breast with Sausage and Apple Stuffing. Invite friends over for Steaks with Zesty Merlot Sauce. Dining this well is just too delicious to call a diet.

Sassy Chicken & Peppers

2 teaspoons Mexican seasoning*
2 (4-ounce) boneless skinless chicken breasts
2 teaspoons canola oil
1 small red onion, sliced
½ red bell pepper, cut into long, thin strips
½ yellow or green bell pepper, cut into long, thin strips
¼ cup chunky salsa or chipotle salsa
1 tablespoon lime juice
  Lime wedges (optional)

*If Mexican seasoning is not available, substitute 1 teaspoon chili powder, ½ teaspoon ground cumin, ½ teaspoon salt and ⅛ teaspoon ground red pepper.

1. Sprinkle seasoning over both sides of chicken.

2. Heat oil in large nonstick skillet over medium heat. Add onion; cook 3 minutes, stirring occasionally.

3. Add bell pepper strips; cook 3 minutes, stirring occasionally.

4. Push vegetables to edges of skillet; add chicken to skillet. Cook 5 minutes; turn. Stir salsa and lime juice into vegetables. Continue to cook 4 minutes or until chicken is no longer pink in the center and vegetables are tender.

5. Transfer chicken to serving plates; top with vegetable mixture and garnish with lime wedges, if desired.   *Makes 2 servings*

Nutrients per Serving (½ of total recipe): Calories: 224, Total Fat: 8 g, Protein: 27 g, Carbohydrate: 11 g, Cholesterol: 69 mg, Sodium: 813 mg, Dietary Fiber: 3 g, Saturated Fat: 1 g

Low-Carb Lasagna

2 medium eggplants (about 1½ pounds total)
1 tablespoon plus 1 teaspoon salt, divided
1½ pounds ground beef
1½ cups meatless pasta sauce (8 or less grams of
 carbohydrate per ½ cup)*
1 teaspoon Italian seasoning
½ teaspoon garlic powder
½ teaspoon pepper
4 cups (2 pounds) whole milk ricotta cheese
1 egg
3 tablespoons chopped parsley, divided
2 cups (8 ounces) shredded mozzarella cheese
¼ cup grated Parmesan cheese

*Check labels carefully. Carbohydrate counts vary greatly.

1. Preheat oven to 350°F. Oil 13×9-inch baking pan. Slice eggplant horizontally into ⅛-inch thick pieces. Layer slices in colander, sprinkling with 1 tablespoon salt. Set aside to drain for at least 20 minutes.

2. Meanwhile cook ground beef in large skillet until no longer pink. Drain fat. Add pasta sauce, Italian seasoning, remaining 1 teaspoon salt, garlic powder and pepper; cook and stir 5 minutes to blend flavors.

3. Spoon ricotta into large bowl. Add egg. With electric mixer beat until light. Mix in 2 tablespoons parsley.

4. Rinse eggplant slices and dry on paper towels. Arrange single layer of eggplant slices in prepared pan. Layer with ½ of ricotta mixture, ½ of meat sauce, ½ of mozzarella and ½ of Parmesan. Arrange eggplant slices over top and layer with remaining ½ of ricotta mixture and ½ of meat sauce. Top with remaining eggplant slices, remaining

86

mozzarella and remaining Parmesan. Sprinkle top with remaining 1 tablespoon parsley.

5. Bake 30 minutes uncovered. Tent loosely with foil and bake additional 10 minutes or until lasagna is heated through and sauce is bubbly. *Makes 15 servings*

Nutrients per Serving: Calories: 314, Total Fat: 21 g, Protein: 21 g, Carbohydrate: 9 g, Cholesterol: 92 mg, Sodium: 494 mg, Dietary Fiber: 4 g, Saturated Fat: 11 g

Low-Carb Lasagna

Moroccan-Style Lamb Chops

1 teaspoon ground cumin
1 teaspoon ground coriander
¾ teaspoon salt
⅛ teaspoon cinnamon
⅛ teaspoon cayenne pepper
1 tablespoon olive oil
2 cloves garlic, minced
4 center cut loin lamb chops, cut 1 inch thick (about
1 pound)

Prepare grill or preheat broiler. In a cup or small bowl, combine cumin, coriander, salt, cinnamon, cayenne pepper and oil; mix well. Rub or brush mixture over both sides of lamb chops. Sprinkle garlic over both sides of lamb chops. Grill on a covered grill or broil 4 to 5 inches from heat source 4 minutes per side for medium-rare or 5 minutes per side for medium.   *Makes 4 servings*

Note: This recipe works well in an indoor countertop grill.

Nutrients per Serving: Calories: 173, Total Fat: 8 g, Protein: 23 g, Carbohydrate: <1 g, Cholesterol: 71 mg, Sodium: 510 mg, Dietary Fiber: <1 g, Saturated Fat: 2 g

Moroccan-Style Lamb Chop

Steaks with Zesty Merlot Sauce

½ **cup merlot wine**
2 **tablespoons Worcestershire sauce**
1 **tablespoon balsamic vinegar**
1 **teaspoon sugar**
1 **teaspoon beef bouillon granules**
½ **teaspoon dried thyme leaves**
2 **beef rib eye steaks (8 ounces each)**
2 **tablespoons finely chopped parsley**

1. Combine wine, Worcestershire sauce, vinegar, sugar, bouillon granules and thyme; set aside.

2. Heat large nonstick skillet over high heat until hot. Add steaks; cook 3 minutes on each side. Turn steaks again and cook 3 to 6 minutes longer over medium heat or until desired doneness.

3. Cut steaks in half; arrange on serving platter. Place in oven to keep warm.

4. Add wine mixture to same skillet. Bring to a boil; cook and stir 1 minute, scraping up any brown bits. Spoon over steaks. Sprinkle with parsley; serve immediately. *Makes 4 servings*

Nutrients per Serving: Calories: 287, Total Fat: 17 g, Protein: 23 g, Carbohydrate: 4 g, Cholesterol: 58 mg, Sodium: 294 mg, Dietary Fiber: <1 g, Saturated Fat: 5 g

Steaks with Zesty Merlot Sauce

Coconut Shrimp with Pear Chutney

Pear chutney (recipe follows)
3 tablespoons unsalted butter
1 pound large raw shrimp, peeled and deveined
½ cup shredded unsweetened coconut flakes
¾ teaspoon curry powder
½ teaspoon salt

1. Preheat oven to 450°F. Prepare Pear Chutney. While it cooks, prepare shrimp.

2. Melt butter in skillet. Remove from heat. Add shrimp and coat with butter. Mix coconut with curry powder and salt in small bowl; spread mixture on dinner plate. Press shrimp into coconut mixture to coat all sides. Place shrimp on cookie sheet.

3. Roast shrimp 4 minutes on first side. Remove from oven, turn over and roast another 2 minutes or until cooked through. Remove from heat immediately. Serve with pear chutney.   *Makes 4 servings*

Nutrients per Serving: Calories: 301, Total Fat: 18 g, Protein: 24 g, Carbohydrate: 11 g, Cholesterol: 197 mg, Sodium: 536 mg, Dietary Fiber: 2 g, Saturated Fat: 9 g

Pear Chutney

 1 tablespoon vegetable oil
 1 jalapeño pepper, seeded and minced*
 1½ teaspoons grated fresh ginger
 1 small shallot, minced
 1 medium unpeeled ripe pear, cut into ½-inch pieces
 1 tablespoon cider vinegar
 1 teaspoon brown sugar
 ⅛ teaspoon salt
 1 tablespoon water
 1 tablespoon chopped green onion

Jalapeño peppers can sting and irritate the skin; wear rubber gloves when handling peppers and do not touch eyes. Wash hands after handling.

1. Heat oil in medium saucepan. Add jalapeño, ginger and shallot. Cook over low heat 5 minutes or until shallot is tender. Add pear, vinegar, brown sugar and salt. Stir in 1 tablespoon water.

2. Cover and cook over low heat 15 minutes or until pear is tender. Stir in green onion and cook 1 minute.   *Makes 4 servings*

Coconut Shrimp with Pear Chutney

Braised Lamb Shanks

2 tablespoons all-purpose flour
1 teaspoon salt
½ teaspoon freshly ground black pepper
4 meaty lamb shanks, about 4 to 5 pounds total
3 tablespoons olive oil, divided
1 tablespoon butter
1 large onion, chopped
4 cloves garlic, minced
1 cup beef or chicken broth
1 cup dry red wine
2 tablespoons chopped fresh rosemary
   Salt and black pepper

1. Preheat oven to 350°F. Combine flour, salt and pepper in a plastic or paper bag. Add shanks to bag one at a time and shake to coat lightly with seasoned flour, using up all of flour mixture.

2. Heat 2 tablespoons oil and butter in a large Dutch oven over medium heat until hot. Add shanks in batches; brown on all sides. Transfer shanks to a plate; set aside. Add remaining 1 tablespoon oil to pan, if needed. Add onion and garlic and cook 5 minutes, stirring frequently. Add broth, wine and rosemary; mix well and bring to a boil over high heat. Return lamb and any accumulated juices to wine mixture. Cover; transfer to oven and braise for 1½ to 2 hours or until shanks are fork tender.

3. Transfer shanks to a serving platter; keep warm. Skim off and discard fat from pan juices. Boil juices gently until reduced to 2 cups and slightly thickened. (Depending on the amount of remaining liquid, this could take from 2 to 10 minutes.) Pour sauce over shanks. Season with salt and pepper to taste.   *Makes 4 servings*

Nutrients per Serving : Calories: 649, Total Fat: 27 g, Protein: 79 g, Carbohydrate: 8 g, Cholesterol: 248 mg, Sodium: 995 mg, Dietary Fiber: <1 g, Saturated Fat: 8 g

Braised Lamb Shanks

Tandoori-Spiced Game Hens

4 cups (32 ounces) plain nonfat yogurt
1 tablespoon curry powder
1 tablespoon sweet paprika
1 teaspoon minced ginger
1 teaspoon minced garlic
4 fresh Cornish game hens, all visible fat removed

1. Mix yogurt with curry powder, paprika, ginger and garlic in large bowl.

2. Cut hens in half by cutting through breast bone. Remove triangular breast bone; discard. Rinse hens.

3. Place hens in resealable plastic food storage bags. Pour yogurt mixture into each bag; seal bags. Marinate in refrigerator 2 to 3 hours or overnight, turning bags once or twice.

4. Preheat oven to 500°F. Remove hens from bags; discard marinade. Lay hens, skin side down on cutting board; brush off excess marinade. Place hens on racks lightly sprayed with nonstick cooking spray. Place racks in shallow baking pans. Bake about 30 to 35 minutes or until no longer pink in center and juices run clear. Garnish, if desired, with fresh celery leaves. *Makes 8 servings*

Note: To keep the hens moist, cook them with the skin on. Remove the skin before serving to keep the fat at 4 grams per serving. With skin, the fat is 24 grams per serving, 7 of which are saturated.

Nutrients per Serving: Calories: 179, Total Fat: 4 g, Protein: 28 g, Carbohydrate: 6 g, Cholesterol: 110 mg, Sodium: 130 mg, Dietary Fiber: <1 g, Saturated Fat: 1 g

Tandoori-Spiced Game Hen

Roast Turkey Breast with Sausage and Apple Stuffing

8 ounces bulk pork sausage
1 medium apple, cored, peeled and finely chopped
1 shallot or small onion, peeled and finely chopped
1 celery stalk, finely chopped
¼ cup chopped hazelnuts
½ teaspoon rubbed sage, divided
½ teaspoon salt, divided
½ teaspoon pepper, divided
1 tablespoon butter
1 turkey breast (4½ to 5 pounds), thawed if frozen
1 cup chicken broth

1. Preheat oven to 325°F. Crumble pork sausage into large skillet. Add apple, shallot and celery. Cook and stir until sausage is cooked through and apple and vegetables are tender. Stir in hazelnuts, ¼ teaspoon sage, ¼ teaspoon salt and ¼ teaspoon pepper.

2. Mash butter with remaining ¼ teaspoon each sage, salt and pepper. Spread over turkey breast. Spoon sausage stuffing into turkey cavity. Close cavity with metal skewers. Place turkey, skin side down, on rack in shallow roasting pan. Pour broth into pan.

3. Roast turkey 45 minutes. Remove turkey from oven, turn skin side up. Baste with broth. Return to oven and roast 1 hour, or until meat thermometer registers 170°F. Remove from oven. Let turkey rest 10 minutes before slicing.   *Makes 6 servings*

Nutrients per Serving: Calories: 724, Total Fat: 39 g, Protein: 80 g, Carbohydrate: 6 g, Cholesterol: 247 mg, Sodium: 727 mg, Dietary Fiber: 1 g, Saturated Fat: 12 g

Roast Turkey Breast with Sausage and Apple Stuffing

Chicken Piccata

   3 tablespoons all-purpose flour
   ½ teaspoon salt
   ¼ teaspoon black pepper
   4 boneless skinless chicken breasts (4 ounces each)
   2 teaspoons olive oil
   1 teaspoon butter
   2 cloves garlic, minced
   ¾ cup fat-free reduced-sodium chicken broth
   1 tablespoon fresh lemon juice
   2 tablespoons chopped Italian parsley
   1 tablespoon drained capers
   Lemon slices and parsley sprigs (optional)

1. Combine flour, salt and pepper in shallow pie plate. Reserve 1 tablespoon of flour mixture.

2. Place chicken between sheets of plastic wrap or waxed paper; pound to ½-inch thickness. Dredge chicken in flour mixture.

3. Heat oil and butter in large nonstick skillet over medium heat until butter is melted. Add chicken; cook 4 to 5 minutes per side or until chicken is cooked through. Transfer chicken to a serving platter; set aside.

4. Add garlic to same skillet; cook and stir over medium heat 1 minute. Add reserved flour mixture; cook and stir 1 minute, stirring constantly. Add broth and lemon juice; simmer, stirring frequently, until sauce thickens, about 2 minutes. Stir in parsley and capers; spoon sauce over chicken. Garnish with lemon slices and parsley sprigs, if desired.   *Makes 4 servings*

Nutrients per Serving: Calories: 194, Total Fat: 6 g, Protein: 27 g, Carbohydrate: 5 g, Cholesterol: 71 mg, Sodium: 473 mg, Dietary Fiber: <1 g, Saturated Fat: 2 g

Chicken Piccata

Pork Curry over Cauliflower Couscous

3 tablespoons olive oil, divided
2 tablespoons mild curry powder
2 teaspoons minced garlic
1½ pounds pork (boneless shoulder, loin or chops), cubed
1 red or green bell pepper, seeded and diced
1 tablespoon cider vinegar
½ teaspoon salt
2 cups water
1 large head cauliflower

1. Heat 2 tablespoons oil over medium heat in large saucepan. Add curry powder and garlic; cook and stir 1 to 2 minutes until garlic is golden.

2. Add pork; stir to coat completely with curry and garlic. Cook and stir 5 to 7 minutes or until pork cubes are barely pink in center. Add bell pepper and vinegar; cook and stir 3 minutes or until bell pepper is soft. Sprinkle with salt.

3. Add water; bring to a boil. Reduce heat and simmer 30 to 45 minutes, stirring occasionally, until liquid is reduced and pork is tender, adding additional water as needed.

4. Meanwhile, trim and core cauliflower; cut into equal pieces. Place in food processor fitted with metal blade. Process using on/off pulsing action until cauliflower is in small uniform pieces about the size of cooked couscous. *Do not purée.*

5. Heat remaining 1 tablespoon oil over medium heat in 12-inch nonstick skillet. Add cauliflower; cook and stir 5 minutes or until cooked crisp-tender. *Do not overcook.* Serve pork curry over cauliflower. *Makes 6 servings*

Nutrients per Serving: Calories: 267, Total Fat: 15 g, Protein: 28 g, Carbohydrate: 7 g, Cholesterol: 69 mg, Sodium: 308 mg, Dietary Fiber: 5 g, Saturated Fat: 10 g

Pork Curry over Cauliflower Couscous

Treat Yourself Right

Go ahead and splurge. Enjoy a rich Chocolate Cannoli or a sensuous slice of Raspberry Cream Pie. You won't be blowing your diet because each of these decadent desserts is less than 16 grams of carbs per serving. What a sweet surprise!

Raspberry Cream Pie

CRUST
- 1⅓ **cups ground pecans**
- 2 **tablespoons melted butter**
- 1 **tablespoon sucralose-based sugar substitute**
- ¼ **teaspoon cinnamon**

FILLING
- ½ **cup water**
- 1 **envelope unflavored gelatin**
- 6 **tablespoons powdered sugar**
- ¼ **cup sucralose-based sugar substitute**
- 1 **tablespoon fresh lemon juice**
- ⅛ **teaspoon salt**
- 2 **cups fresh raspberries or 1 bag (12 ounces) frozen unsweetened raspberries, thawed**
- 1 **cup heavy cream**

1. Preheat oven to 350°F. Combine ground pecans, melted butter, sugar substitute and cinnamon in medium bowl. Press into bottom and up sides of 9-inch pie plate. Bake 5 to 7 minutes or until the crust is set and lightly browned. Remove from oven and cool completely.

2. Pour ½ cup water into medium saucepan. Sprinkle with gelatin. Set aside 5 minutes to dissolve gelatin. Add powdered sugar, sugar substitute, lemon juice and salt. Simmer until sugar dissolves. Stir in raspberries. Set aside until thickened, about 30 minutes. Whip cream in electric mixer until stiff peaks form. Fold in raspberry mixture. Gently spoon into prepared crust. Chill 2 to 3 hours before serving.

Makes 8 servings

Nutrients per Serving: Calories: 299, Total Fat: 27 g, Protein: 3 g, Carbohydrate: 14 g, Cholesterol: 49 mg, Sodium: 81 mg, Dietary Fiber: 4 g, Saturated Fat: 10 g

Milk Chocolate Frozen Mousse

1½ **cups heavy cream, divided**
½ **cup water**
1 **envelope unflavored gelatin**
6 **tablespoons powdered sugar**
2 **tablespoons unsweetened cocoa powder**
½ **teaspoon ground cinnamon**
¼ **teaspoon salt**
2 **tablespoons sucralose-based sugar substitute**
1 **teaspoon vanilla extract**
3 **tablespoons honey-roasted sliced almonds**

1. Combine ½ cup cream and water in small saucepan. Sprinkle with gelatin. Set aside 5 minutes to soften. Stir in powdered sugar, cocoa, cinnamon and salt. Stir over low heat until cocoa is blended and gelatin dissolves. Remove from heat and cool slightly. Stir in sugar substitute and vanilla.

2. Chill gelatin mixture 1 hour or until partially set. Pour remaining 1 cup cream into bowl of electric mixer. Beat to form stiff peaks. Gently fold chocolate mixture into cream. Spoon into 2-quart soufflé or casserole dish. Sprinkle with sliced almonds. Place in freezer 1 hour or until semi-frozen. *Makes 6 servings*

Nutrients per Serving (½ cup): Calories: 275, Total Fat: 25 g, Protein: 3 g, Carbohydrate: 12 g, Cholesterol: 82 mg, Sodium: 129 mg, Dietary Fiber: 1 g, Saturated Fat: 14 g

Milk Chocolate Frozen Mousse

No-Bake Blueberry Cheesecake

CRUST
   1 tablespoon butter
   8 zwieback toasts*

FILLING
   1 envelope unflavored gelatin
   1 cup boiling water
   2 packages (16 ounces) cream cheese, softened
   ⅓ cup sucralose-based sugar substitute
   1 teaspoon vanilla extract
   1 cup thawed whipped topping
   ¾ cup unsweetened frozen blueberries

*Zwieback toast can be found in the baby food aisle of most grocery stores.

1. Add boiling water to gelatin and stir until dissolved; set aside.

2. Place zwieback toasts and 1 tablespoon butter in food processor; pulse until coarse crumbs form. Pat thin layer of crumbs in bottom of 9-inch springform pan.

3. Beat cream cheese, sugar substitute and vanilla on medium speed in large bowl of electric mixer until well blended. Beat in whipped topping. Add dissolved gelatin in steady stream while beating on slow speed. Mixture will become loose and lumpy. Beat 4 minutes on medium speed until smooth and creamy, scraping side of bowl occasionally.

4. Fold in frozen blueberries; pour into prepared pan. Refrigerate 3 hours or until set. *Makes 8 servings*

Nutrients per Serving: Calories: 284, Total Fat: 24 g, Protein: 6 g, Carbohydrate: 11 g, Cholesterol: 66 mg, Sodium: 196 mg, Dietary Fiber: 1 g, Saturated Fat: 15 g

No-Bake Blueberry Cheesecake

Cheese Blintzes with Strawberries & Sour Cream

3 tablespoons melted butter, divided
1 container (15 ounces) whole-milk ricotta cheese
**1 tablespoon plus 2 teaspoons powdered sugar substitute,
  divided**
1 teaspoon vanilla
⅛ teaspoon ground nutmeg
8 (8-inch) prepared crêpes
½ cup sliced fresh strawberries
¼ cup sour cream

1. Preheat oven to 350°F. Brush 1 tablespoon butter over bottom of 13×9-inch baking dish.

2. Combine cheese, 1 tablespoon sugar substitute, vanilla and nutmeg in food processor; process until smooth. Spoon scant ¼ cup mixture onto center of each crêpe. Fold outside edges of crêpe over filling; roll up from bottom. Place crêpes, seam side down, in prepared dish. Brush remaining 2 tablespoons butter over crêpes. Bake uncovered 18 to 20 minutes or until hot.

3. Meanwhile, combine strawberries and remaining 2 teaspoons sugar substitute; set aside at room temperature. Transfer crêpes to serving plates; top with strawberries. Serve with sour cream.

Makes 4 servings

Tip: Look for shelf-stable packages of crêpes near the berries in the supermarket produce section.

Nutrients per Serving: Calories: 362, Total Fat: 27 g, Protein: 15 g, Carbohydrate: 16 g, Cholesterol: 94 mg, Sodium: 289 mg, Dietary Fiber: <1 g, Saturated Fat: 15 g

Cheese Blintzes with Strawberries & Sour Cream

Coconut Flan

3 tablespoons water
1 envelope unflavored gelatin
1 can (14½ ounces) unsweetened coconut milk
8 packets sucralose-based sugar substitute
2 tablespoons powdered sugar
½ teaspoon vanilla
4 tablespoons toasted flaked coconut
2 (½ inch thick) slices fresh pineapple, cut into bite-size pieces

1. Place water in small bowl and sprinkle gelatin over top; set aside.

2. Place coconut milk, sugar substitute, powdered sugar and vanilla in medium saucepan. Heat over medium heat, stirring to dissolve sugar and smooth out coconut milk. *Do not boil.* Add gelatin mixture and stir until gelatin is dissolved.

3. Pour into 4 custard cups and chill until set, about 3 hours. To unmold, run a thin blade around inside edge of cups and place bottoms in hot water for about 30 seconds. Place serving plate over cup, invert and shake until flan drops onto plate. Top each flan with 1 tablespoon toasted coconut and arrange ¼ of pineapple pieces on plate. Refrigerate leftovers promptly and eat within 2 days.

Makes 4 servings

Nutrients per Serving: Calories: 261, Total Fat: 24 g, Protein: 4 g, Carbohydrate: 13 g, Cholesterol: 0 mg, Sodium: 18 mg, Dietary Fiber: 1 g, Saturated Fat: 21 g

Coconut Flan

Chocolate Fondue with Fresh Fruit

3 tablespoons unsweetened cocoa
1 cup heavy cream, divided
4 ounces (½ cup) cream cheese, cut in chunks
3 tablespoons plus 1 teaspoon sucralose-based sugar substitute
½ teaspoon vanilla
24 green or red seedless grapes
12 small to medium strawberries, halved, or 6 large strawberries, quartered

1. In a small saucepan or fondue pot over low heat, combine cocoa with ½ cup cream and whisk to mix completely. When cream-cocoa mixture is hot and thick, add remaining cream and cream cheese and cook, stirring constantly, until mixture is smooth and thick. Add sucralose and vanilla, stirring to mix.

2. Transfer mixture to holder with warmer candle and keep warm over very low heat. Arrange strawberries and grapes on a plate. Provide each guest with a 7-inch long wooden skewer or a fondue fork for dipping.   *Makes 8 servings*

Note: Substitute fruit in season for the grapes and strawberries.

Nutrients per Serving (6 pieces fruit plus 3 tablespoons fondue):
Calories: 177, Total Fat: 16 g, Protein: 2 g, Carbohydrate: 7 g,
Cholesterol: 57 mg, Sodium: 55 mg, Dietary Fiber: 1 g,
Saturated Fat: 10 g

Chocolate Fondue with Fresh Fruit

Ricotta Cheese & Blueberry Parfaits

1 cup whole milk ricotta cheese
1 tablespoon powdered sugar
Grated peel of 1 lemon
1½ cups fresh blueberries
Chopped pecans or slivered almonds (optional)

1. Combine ricotta cheese, sugar and lemon peel in medium bowl; stir well.

2. Place 3 tablespoons blueberries in each of 4 parfait glasses. Add ¼ cup ricotta cheese mixture; top with another 3 tablespoons blueberries. Sprinkle with chopped pecans or slivered almonds., if desired. *Makes 4 servings*

Nutrients per Serving (⅔ cup): Calories: 145, Total Fat: 8 g, Protein: 7 g, Carbohydrate: 12 g, Cholesterol: 31 mg, Sodium: 55 mg, Dietary Fiber: 2 g, Saturated Fat: 5 g

Some recipes in this book use small amounts of regular sugar instead of, or in addition to, sugar substitute. In most cases the flavor difference from adding regular sugar was felt to be worth the additional carbohydrates. You can use the sugar substitute of your choice, if you prefer. In recipes for baked goods, however, substitutions can effect the texture of the final dish, in addition to its flavor.

Ricotta Cheese & Blueberry Parfaits

Orange-Scented Panna Cotta

2 tablespoons orange-flavored liqueur or orange juice
1 envelope unflavored gelatin
3 cups heavy cream
¼ cup powdered sugar
2 tablespoons sucralose-based sugar substitute
1 teaspoon finely grated orange peel
½ teaspoon vanilla

1. Combine liqueur and gelatin in a cup. Set aside 10 minutes without stirring. Gelatin will absorb liquid.

2. Combine cream, sugar, sugar substitute and orange peel in heavy-bottomed pot. Bring to a simmer, stirring constantly over medium heat. Add gelatin mixture and simmer 1 minute more, stirring constantly, to dissolve gelatin. Remove from heat and stir in vanilla.

3. Spoon cream mixture into 6 custard cups. Set aside 30 minutes to cool. Refrigerate 3 to 4 hours.

4. To serve, run a knife around the inside edge of each cup. Invert cups onto serving plates.   *Makes 6 servings*

Nutrients per Serving (½ cup): Calories: 454, Total Fat: 44 g, Protein: 3 g, Carbohydrate: 10 g, Cholesterol: 164 mg, Sodium: 48 mg, Dietary Fiber: <1 g, Saturated Fat: 28 g

Orange-Scented Panna Cotta

Chocolate Cannoli

1 cup heavy cream
1 ounce (1 square) unsweetened chocolate
⅔ cup sucralose-based sugar substitute
⅓ cup whole milk ricotta cheese
1 teaspoon vanilla or almond extract
¼ teaspoon salt
8 unfilled cannoli shells (½ ounce each)*
1 teaspoon miniature chocolate chips or crushed pistachio nuts (optional)

*Cannoli shells can be found at Italian bakeries and delis or in ethnic food aisles at some supermarkets. If shells are unavailable, serve filling in dessert dish with sugar wafer or other cookie.

1. With an electric mixer, whip cream until stiff peaks form. Set aside.

2. Place chocolate in small microwavable bowl and microwave at HIGH 30 seconds. Stir, and if necessary, continue microwaving and stirring at 30-second intervals until chocolate is melted.

3. Combine sugar substitute, ricotta, vanilla and salt in medium bowl. Stir in melted chocolate. Fold reserved whipped cream into mixture.

4. Spoon or pipe ¼ cup mixture into each cannoli shell. Garnish with chocolate chips or crushed pistachio nuts, if desired.

Makes 8 servings

Nutrients per Serving (1 cannoli): Calories: 230, Total Fat: 18 g, Protein: 3 g, Carbohydrate: 12 g, Cholesterol: 46 mg, Sodium: 23 mg, Dietary Fiber: 1 g, Saturated Fat: 10 g

Chocolate Cannoli

Index

Acknowledgments

The publisher would like to thank the companies and organizations listed below for the use of their recipes and photographs in this publication.

Del Monte Corporation

Equal® sweetener

Wisconsin Milk Marketing Board

METRIC CONVERSION CHART

VOLUME MEASUREMENTS (dry)

$1/8$ teaspoon = 0.5 mL
$1/4$ teaspoon = 1 mL
$1/2$ teaspoon = 2 mL
$3/4$ teaspoon = 4 mL
1 teaspoon = 5 mL
1 tablespoon = 15 mL
2 tablespoons = 30 mL
$1/4$ cup = 60 mL
$1/3$ cup = 75 mL
$1/2$ cup = 125 mL
$2/3$ cup = 150 mL
$3/4$ cup = 175 mL
1 cup = 250 mL
2 cups = 1 pint = 500 mL
3 cups = 750 mL
4 cups = 1 quart = 1 L

VOLUME MEASUREMENTS (fluid)

1 fluid ounce (2 tablespoons) = 30 mL
4 fluid ounces ($1/2$ cup) = 125 mL
8 fluid ounces (1 cup) = 250 mL
12 fluid ounces ($1^1/2$ cups) = 375 mL
16 fluid ounces (2 cups) = 500 mL

WEIGHTS (mass)

$1/2$ ounce = 15 g
1 ounce = 30 g
3 ounces = 90 g
4 ounces = 120 g
8 ounces = 225 g
10 ounces = 285 g
12 ounces = 360 g
16 ounces = 1 pound = 450 g

DIMENSIONS

$1/16$ inch = 2 mm
$1/8$ inch = 3 mm
$1/4$ inch = 6 mm
$1/2$ inch = 1.5 cm
$3/4$ inch = 2 cm
1 inch = 2.5 cm

OVEN TEMPERATURES

250°F = 120°C
275°F = 140°C
300°F = 150°C
325°F = 160°C
350°F = 180°C
375°F = 190°C
400°F = 200°C
425°F = 220°C
450°F = 230°C

BAKING PAN SIZES

Utensil	Size in Inches/Quarts	Metric Volume	Size in Centimeters
Baking or Cake Pan (square or rectangular)	8×8×2	2 L	20×20×5
	9×9×2	2.5 L	23×23×5
	12×8×2	3 L	30×20×5
	13×9×2	3.5 L	33×23×5
Loaf Pan	8×4×3	1.5 L	20×10×7
	9×5×3	2 L	23×13×7
Round Layer Cake Pan	8×1½	1.2 L	20×4
	9×1½	1.5 L	23×4
Pie Plate	8×1¼	750 mL	20×3
	9×1¼	1 L	23×3
Baking Dish or Casserole	1 quart	1 L	—
	1½ quart	1.5 L	—
	2 quart	2 L	—